2nd Edition

ALL ARE WELCOME! FEEL THE SPIRIT!

Eight World Music Choral Anthems for Youth, Adults and Congregation

Music by Dr. Abe Cáceres

worldhousemusic
www.worldhousemusic.org

worldhousemusic
www.worldhousemusic.org
© 2019 World House Music, Inc

ISBN 978-1-930099-07-4

January, 2019

Brothers & Sisters,

Intergenerational communication affirms family and community. This collection of flexible mixed voice anthems provides opportunities for children, youth, and adults to participate in fun, intergenerational music making. Together with the congregation, the entire worshiping body contributes to the musical offering. This collection has elements of European music, ragtime, Afro-Latin rhythms, jazz, Black Gospel, and holy hip hop – something for everyone! The scores include instructional details and suggestions for percussion, piano and organ. Visit our website to download lead sheets for congregational use, as well.

In the Contents and Notes section of the book you will find the lyrics of the anthems, and fascinating cultural, historical and compositional information about each number. The Contents and Notes section is also posted on our website.

In this edition, typographical errors from the first edition have been corrected. Some performance suggestions have also been added. If you have a copy of the second edition, you may download a list of errata from the WHM website. Please note these related resources available via the WHM website:

- All Are Welcome! Feel the Spirit! - CD
- All Are Welcome! Feel the Spirit! - Accompaniment performance Tracks

May the current collection help us proclaim, *"All Are Welcome! Feel the Spirit!"*

World House Music promotes cross-cultural communication and healing through interactive programs of world music in schools, churches, and interfaith venues.
Please support our mission with tax deductable donations online or by mail.

worldhousemusic

www.worldhousemusic.org

Acknowledgements

The idea of this collection of anthems came from my wife, Mila. She has been at times my eyes, ears, hands, and heart. She helped make it a reality, and I know she is also glad that it is finished! My greatest debt is to her. But my daughter, Elise, and son, Sol, assisted in ways as mundane as collating, and as technical as Facebook issues. Mr. John Mason has spent many hours reworking the web site. He was also our contact person to Ms. Darany Samountry, who designed the new logo. Another talented graphic artist, Mr. Stephen Stoffel, designed the book cover. The photos are the gifts of Ms. Jeanne Mueller, Rev. Ed Ruen, Mr. Randy Stubbs, and Mr. Ron Quimby.

I am grateful to the World House Music Board of Directors, Rev. Oscar Kraft, Mr. Paul Kwiecien and Rev. Dr. Tim Perkins for constant support and energy. Members of the Advisory Board of Directors, Mr. Abdulhamid Alwan, Mr. Jim Sherman, Dr. John McDowell, Dr. Jonathan Shutman, Ms. Mary Campbell, and Mr. Mike Reyes, have all been available to me. Their thoughts and support have helped shape this volume. Mr. Dave Klitz has been my "go-to guy" for all things accounting.

Several people have reviewed the manuscript and given many suggestions and corrections. Among those are Mr. J. Mark Baker, Dr. Wallace Cheatham, Ms. Rebecca Ferguson, Mr. Miguel de Jesús, Ms. Penny Schwid, and Rev. Tim Tahtinen. Thanks to to Ms. Sarah Howden for editing the 2nd edition, and to Rev. Wesley Spears-Newsome for contributing his graphic art skills. Many others have contributed in myriad ways – you will see some of their names in the pages that follow.

I've had many mentors throughout the way. The first and most important, of course, were Mom and Dad. Then there was Paco, who on a hot summer day, on a bench in a New York City housing project, introduced me to conga drumming. I was a kid, and never got his last name. My first piano teacher, Ms. Ida N. Wellerson, nurtured a fragile spirit, and my last piano teacher, Prof. Frederick Marvin, taught me how to play more passionately than I could imagine. Others include Prof. Umberto Pisani, Mr. Dan Barahanos, Mr. Myron Jones, Mr. Frank C. Smith, Mr. Alexander Richter, Dr. Earl George, Dr. Abe Veinus, Dean Howard Boatwright, and Dr. George List. Each of them left their mark on me. There is no way to pay the debt except to pass the agape forward.

Finally, thanks to you all for participating in this journey with me!

Peblejah!

Abe Cáceres

PS: Peblejah = PEace, BLEssings, Justice, Agape, Hope. (This is an "aberism.")

Contents
and Notes

1. All Are Welcome in this Place
Unison or two part mixed
Biblical references: Psalm 133:1-3,
Romans 12:9-11, Ephesians 2:4-18

 *Lyrics*

1. All Are Welcome in this Place
All Are Welcome in this Place.

Refrain
Each of us has a space
Because God's amazing grace
  turns sinners into saints in this place.
Yes, grace turns sinners into saints in this
place.

2. All Are Welcome have no fear.
You won't be judged; we're all sinners here.
Refrain

3. All Are Welcome, say "Amen!" "Amen!"
Come and never be lonely again!
Refrain

Bridge
Amazing Grace! How sweet the sound

That saved a wretch like me!
I once was lost, but now I'm found.
Was blind, but now I see.

1. All Are Welcome in this Place
All Are Welcome in this Place.
Refrain

Lyrics and Music © 2012 World House Music
www.worldhousemusic.org

This is high energy anthem
has an easy, catchy refrain.
Originally composed for All
Saint's Day, it is appropriate for any
Sunday with an emphasis on the
community, or the power of God's
grace. The middle section consists
of an upbeat setting of the first verse
of *Amazing Grace.*

All Are Welcome in this Place was
inspired by a recording I heard of
Sister Arizona Dranes playing her
own compositions. Sister Arizona
was one of the first great Gospel
pianists of the 1920's. Born in
Texas, she was blind, and believed
to be of mixed Mexican and African
American heritage. She brought the
ragtime piano style of secular
world into the COGIC (Church of
God in Christ) church and beyond.
This was extremely controversial
because ragtime and blues were
considered "the Devil's music."

Elements of "rag piano" are
incorporated in this song, along with
a walking bass. Advanced pianists
may wish to download from our web
site the piano score used for the CD.

2. El Bautismo (Baptism)
SA/SAB/ SATB
Biblical references: Mathew 3:1-6,
13-17; John 8:32; Colossians 2:12

 *Lyrics*

Refrain
El Bautismo! O! El Bautismo!

1. John proclaimed, "The Kingdom of
Heaven is at hand."
And many came to be baptized from
throughout Judea land.   Por eso [that's why]
Refrain

2. Jesus came to be baptized, the Spirit
came as a Dove.
"This is the One with whom I am pleased,"
came the voice from up above. Por eso…
Refrain

Bridge
So we baptize in the name of the Creator!
We baptize in the name of the Son!
We baptize in the name of the Spirit!
We baptize every one!
Refrain

3. Baptized to life into community.
Feel the Spirit, live the Word,
And the Truth will set you free! Por eso
Refrain

Lyrics and Music © 2011 World House Music
www.worldhousemusic.org

This joyful choral number is in a Puerto Rican style known as *plena.* The lyrics outline the story of baptism from the time of John the Baptist, Jesus' baptism, and the meaning of baptism as the symbol of membership into the community of faith.

This song was originally composed for my daughter's *Quinceañera*, the Latin American tradition of celebrating the transition of life of a girl into adulthood. In Christian circles, the event emphasizes the confirmation of baptism.

Percussion instruction and tips for the pianist will be available on-line. The *plena* is both a song form and a dance. You can see the dance steps to this song on YouTube via a link from www.worldhousemusic.org.

Thanks to my brother José Antonio Machado for ideas and musical suggestions.

3. Emmanuel Joy
SAB/SATB with rap choir
Biblical references: Mathew 1:19-23;
2:13

 *Lyrics*
Refrain
Emmanuel. Emmanuel.
His name is called Emmanuel.
God with us. Emmanuel.
His name is called Emmanuel!

1. God came down on earth to dwell
As Jesus, Emmanuel.
Came to show us how to live,
How to love, how to forgive!
Refrain

2. Mary's pregnant! Who's to blame?
Joseph would not cause her shame.
Dream-time angel came to say,
"The child comes by mysterious way.

A Spirit child! Give him a home.
Adopt the child, call him your own.
Tell no one from whence he came;
And Jesus is to be his name."
Refrain

3. Joseph, Mary, baby, three
Fled King Herod's tyranny.
Escaped to Egypt secretly:
Holy family, refugee.

Adopted, immigrant, refugee,
Healer, scholar, He would be.
Loved all people equally,
Fisherman, Pharisee,

(Child) Even folks like you and me?
(Adult) Even folks like you and me!
Refrain

Lyrics and Music © 2012 World House Music
www.worldhousemusic.org

 This Christmas anthem truly speaks to young people, both in style and content. Influenced by contemporary *Holy Hip Hop*, rap verses talk about social and justice themes inherent in the Christmas story that are as relevant today as ever: teen pregnancy outside of marriage, shame, adoption, immigration, refugee status.

The refrain expresses the joy of Christmas, and the hope and wholeness of spirit that comes with Emmanuel, "God with us."

4. Enviado Soy de Dios – Each One of Us is Sent
SAB/SATB with congregation
Biblical Reference: James 2:14-17

Lyrics
Enviado soy de Dios,
mi mano lista está
para construir con él
un mundo fraternal.

Los ángeles no son
enviados a cambiar
un mundo de dolor
por un mundo mejor;
me ha tocado a mí
hacerlo realidad.
Ayúdame, Señor,
a hacer tu voluntad.

Literal Translation
I am sent by God.
My hand is ready
to build with God
a fraternal world.

Angles are not sent
to change a painful world
into a better world.
It's up to me
to make it reality.
Help me, Lord,
to do your will.

Singable Translation
Each one of us is sent,
is sent by God above,
to do our very best,
to be agape love.

The angels are not sent
to do what we can do,
to make a better world
for all, not just a few.
It's up to you and me
to make the dream come true.
We pray to you, O Lord,
to show us what to do.

Spanish lyrics and music traditional Central America
English translation and arrangement with original material, Abe Cáceres
© 2012 World House Music

This is a social protest song from Central America with roots in the church. The musical arrangement is a fusion of Central American folk protest song style usually played with guitar, and Andean Aymara folk music. Scored for pan pipes or flutes, guitar and/or piano, bass and percussion, this arrangement is also effective with organ, guitar, bass and percussion.

5. Fruit of the Spirit
SAB/SATB
Galations 5:22-23

 *Lyrics*
Refrain
Love. Joy. Peace.
Patience. Kindness. Goodness.
Faithfulness. Gentleness. Self-control.
Such are the fruit of the Spirit.

Love. Joy. Peace.
Patience. Kindness. Goodness.
Faithfulness. Gentleness. Self-control.
Against these there is no law.

Bridge
These are the fruit of the Spirit
If we live in the Spirit,
Let us walk in the Spirit.
Love you neighbor as you love yourself
And there will be….
Refrain

Lyrics and Music © 2012 World House Music
www.worldhousemusic.org

Biblical text couched in a memorable melody can become part of one's conscious and subconscious mind. This jazz waltz will have the text of the Fruit of the Spirit dancing in the minds of children, youth and adults. This is a great New Testament text for interfaith events. "Against these, there is no law."

6. I Am Available to You, O Lord
Unison or two part mixed choir
Biblical reference: Isaiah 64:8

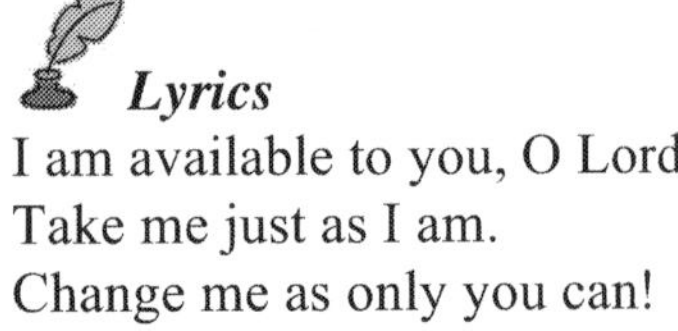 *Lyrics*
I am available to you, O Lord
Take me just as I am.
Change me as only you can!

Make me a part of your plan!
I am available to you, O Lord.

Lyrics and Music © 2006 World House Music
www.worldhousemusic.org

 This anthem is designed to be sung as a part of a prayer. Composed in a Nat King Cole jazz piano style, the prayers are nestled between two reflective submissions to God's will. It can be sung, however, as an anthem without the prayer.

7. Somos Uno – We Are One
Unison/SA/SAB/SATB with congregation
Biblical Reference: Ephesians 4:2-6

Lyrics
Somos uno, en Cristo somos uno.
Somos uno, uno somos.

Un solo Dios,
Un solo Señor,
Una sola fe,
Un solo amor,
Un solo bautismo,
Un solo espíritu,
Ese es El Consolador!

Singable translation
We are one in Christ Jesus
We're united. We're united
We're united!

We have one God.
We have one Lord.
We have one faith.
We have one love.
We have on baptism.
We have one Spirit.
It is God, the Comforter!

Melody and Spanish lyrics, traditional pan Latin

American collected, transcribed and translated and copyrighted by Abe Cáceres in 1985. Choral arrangement © 2000 World House Music

 This exciting song is in essence a creed. It can be played as a Puerto Rican *plena*, like *El Bautismo*, or as a *merengue*, a rhythm associated with the Dominican Republic. The difference is in the percussion accompaniment. Visit our web site to hear a version of *Somos Uno*, as *plena*, and one as *merengue*. Visit our web site for more information about percussion.

The middle section consists of the words "we are one" translated into various languages, and layered one upon another. This is a great opportunity to express unity as well as to simulate the spirit of Pentecost!

The melodic setting of each language reflects the culture and is accompanied by an instrument of that culture. In the basic arrangement the following four languages are represented.

1. German is accompanied by accordion in a polka style.

2. Chinese is accompanied by a Chinese pitch-changing gong. The first part of the melody follows the tones of Mandarin Chinese.

3. Arabic is accompanied by a Middle Eastern drum called *Arabic tabla* and oboe known as *zurna*. The melody includes the augmented 2nd, characteristic of the region.

4. Swahili is accompanied by a Tanzanian shaker, and the melody is set to a syncopated rhythm.

Other languages with melodies which can be layered upon each other are offered in the book and on our web site. In the CD recording Swedish, Pilipino, Japanese and Twi are used. Feel free to compose your own melodies with languages that reflect your region or area of ministry, or contact Dr. Abe to compose one for your congregation.

8. This is the Day
Unison or SAB
Biblical references: Psalms 118:24 and 24:1

 Lyrics
Refrain
This is the day! This is the day!
This is the day that the Lord has made!
Let us rejoice and be glad in it!
This is the Day of the Lord!

Bridge
The earth is the Lord's
and the fullness thereof,
and all, all, all they that dwell therein! Yes!
Refrain

(All SHOUT)
REJOICE! REJOICE! REJOICE!

Lyrics and Music © 2007 World House Music
www.worldhousemusic.org

Composed as a high energy call to worship for the Easter season, this anthem can be used any time a joyous affirmation of life is in order. In a Black Gospel style with walking bass and a stick-to-your-mind melody, children love the ending, because it is one of the few times that they are actually encouraged to shout in church!

All Are Welcome in This Place

Unison or 2 Part Choir and Congregation

Abe Cáceres

worldhousemusic

6

All Are Welcome in This Place

All Are Welcome in This Place

D.C. al Coda

once was lost, but now I'm found. Was blind, but now I see.
place. Yes, grace turns sin-ners in-to saints in this place.

El Bautismo - Baptism

SAB/SATB, Youth Choir and Congregation

Abe Cáceres

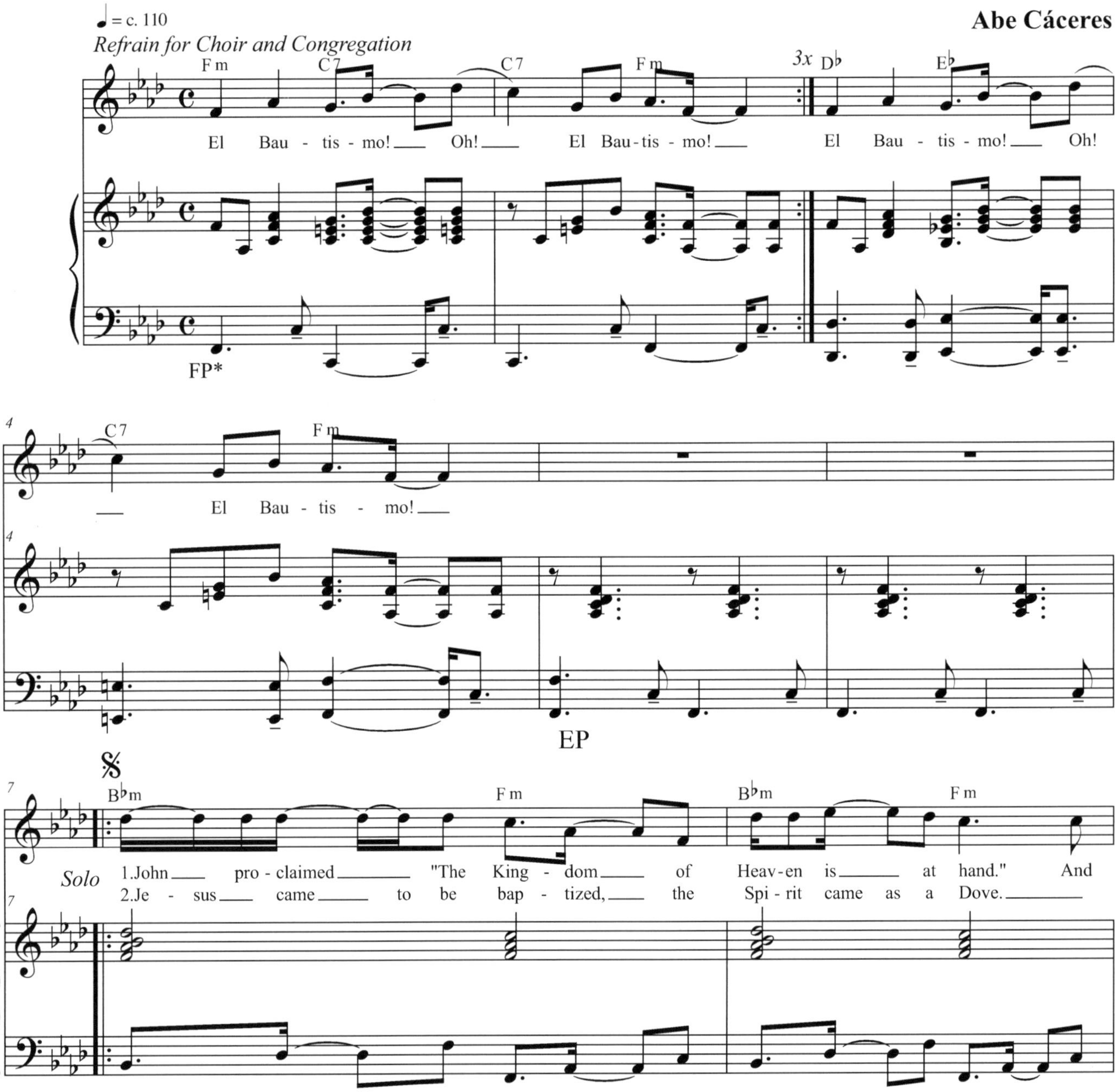

*FP = Full Percussion   NP = No Percussion

EP = Edit Percussion, eg: no small percussion, or drop out the bell, or just use maracas.

Visit www.worldhousemusic.org for additional details.

10

El Bautismo - Baptism

El Bautismo - Baptism

*If the descant is not sung at mm 45 and 71, then omit mm 33-36

El Bautismo - Baptism

El Bautismo - Baptism

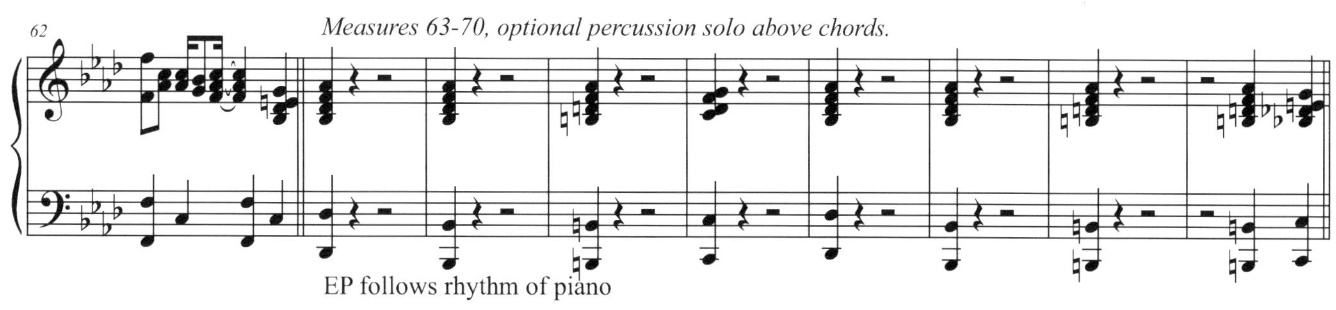

El Bautismo - Baptism

Emmanuel Joy

SAB/SATB, Youth Rap Choir and Congregation

Abe Cáceres

Emmanuel Joy
God with us, Em-man-u-el. His name is called Em-man-u-el!
God with us, Em-man-u-el.
F 6 G 6 Em7 Am Dm7 Dm7/G C C/B♭
His name is called Em-man-u-el!
Em-
C/A C/G F C/E F/E♭ Dm7/G C F 13 F♯13 F 13 F♯13 G 13 C 9 F 13 F♯13 G 13
1. 2.
man - u - el. Em - man - u - el. Em-
C 9
Percussion continues.. etc.

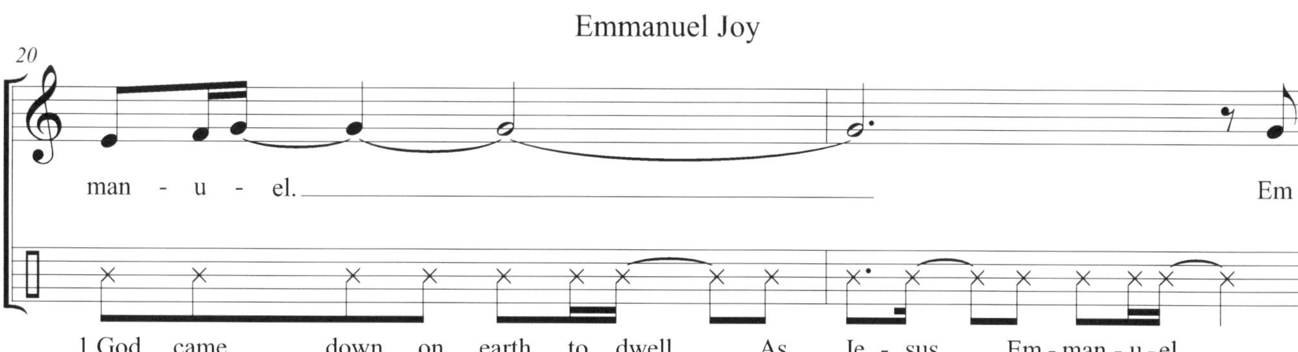
20
man - u - el. ________ Em -
1.God came down on earth to dwell____ As Je - sus____ Em - man - u - el.

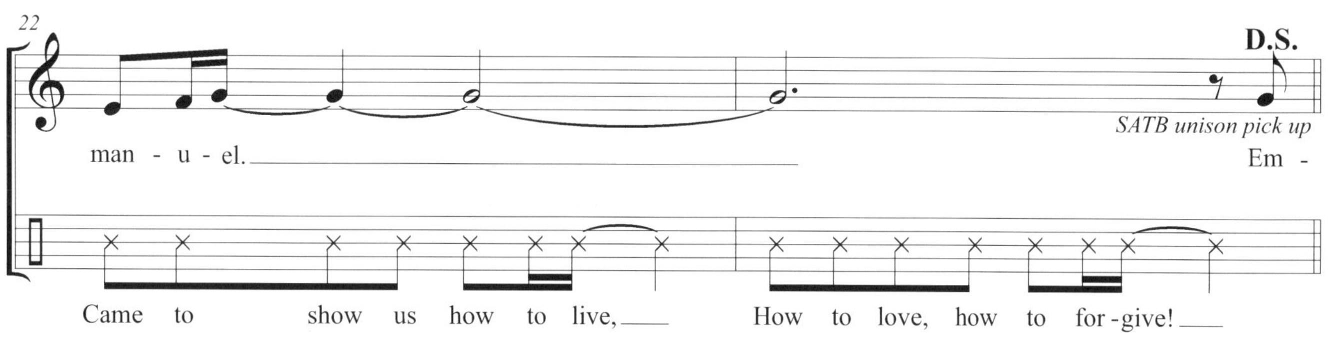
22
D.S.
SATB unison pick up
man - u - el. ________ Em -
Came to show us how to live,____ How to love, how to for-give!____

24
3.
Em - man-u - el.________ Em - man-u - el.________
24
F 13 F#13 G 13   C 9 F 13 F#13 G 13   C 9

29
___ Em - man - u - el. ________ Em-
2.Ma-ry's preg-nant! Who's to blame?____ Jo-seph would not cause her shame.____

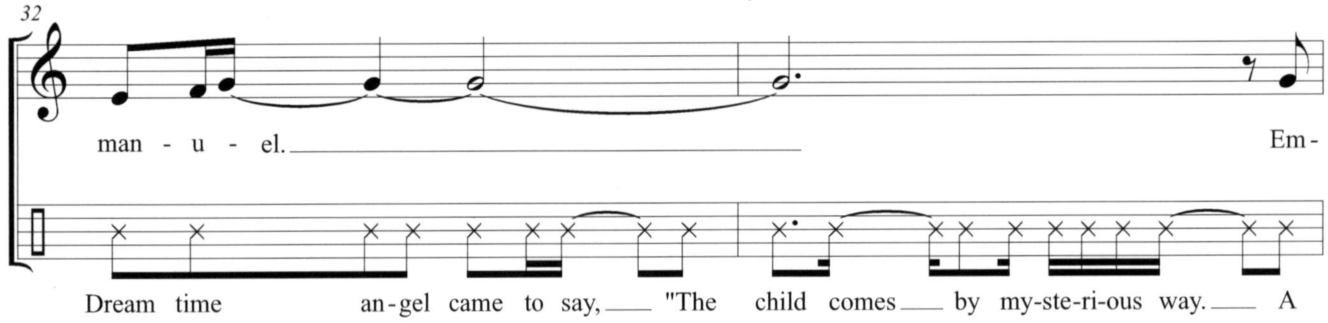
32
man - u - el.
Em-
Dream time an-gel came to say, "The child comes by my-ste-ri-ous way. A

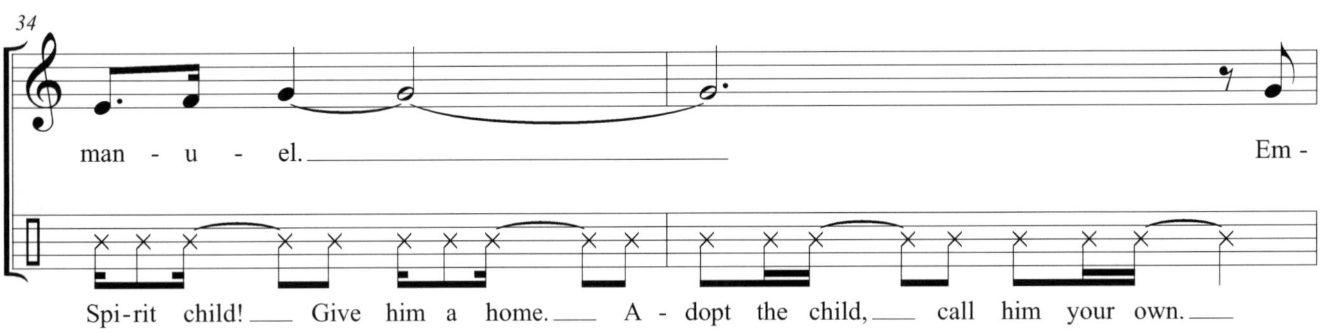
34
man - u - el.
Em -
Spi-rit child! Give him a home. A - dopt the child, call him your own.

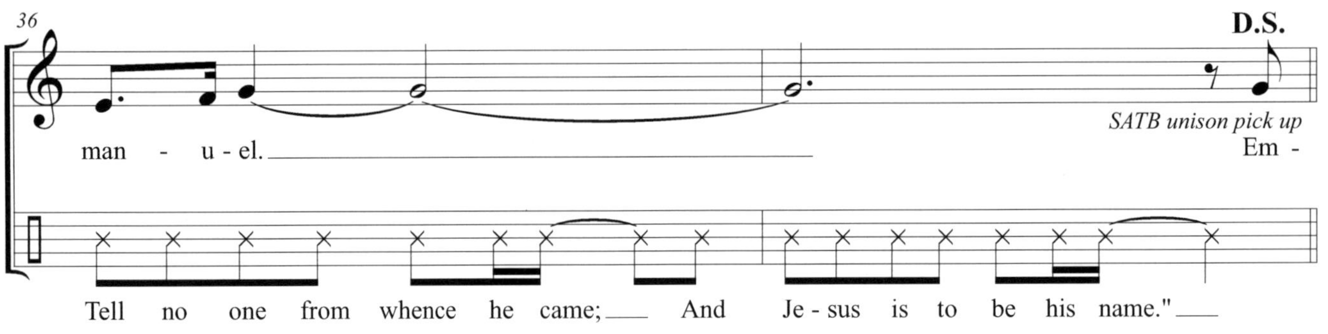
36
D.S.
SATB unison pick up
man - u - el.
Em -
Tell no one from whence he came; And Je - sus is to be his name."

38
4.
Em - man - u - el.
Em-
38
F 13 F#13 G 13 C 9 F 13 F#13 G 13 C 9

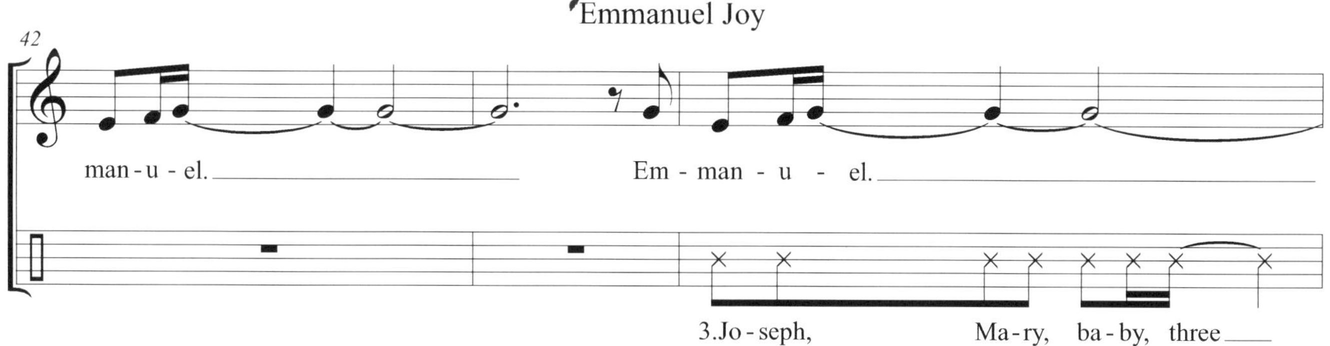

Emmanuel Joy
42
man - u - el.
Em - man - u - el.
3.Jo - seph,
Ma - ry, ba - by, three

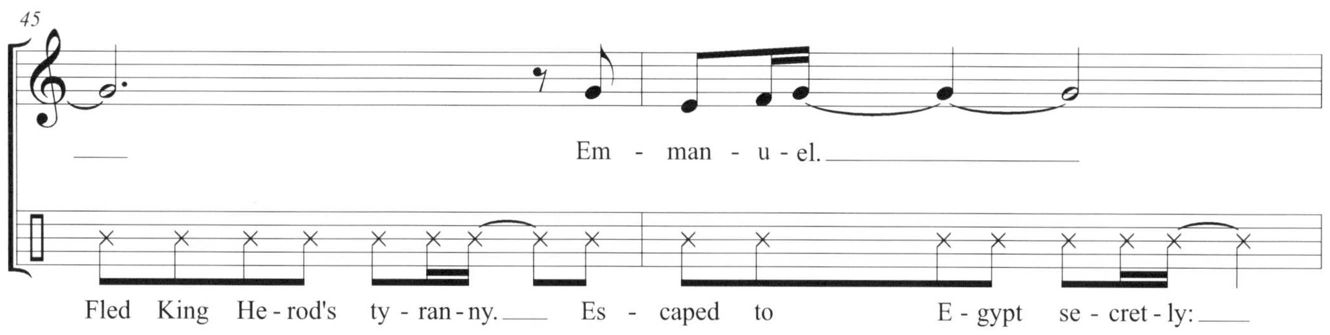

45
Em - man - u - el.
Fled King He - rod's ty - ran - ny. Es - caped to E - gypt se - cret - ly:

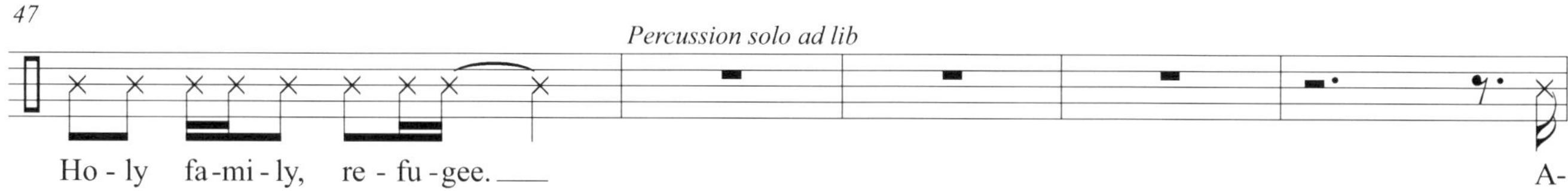

47
Percussion solo ad lib
Ho - ly fa - mi - ly, re - fu - gee.
A-

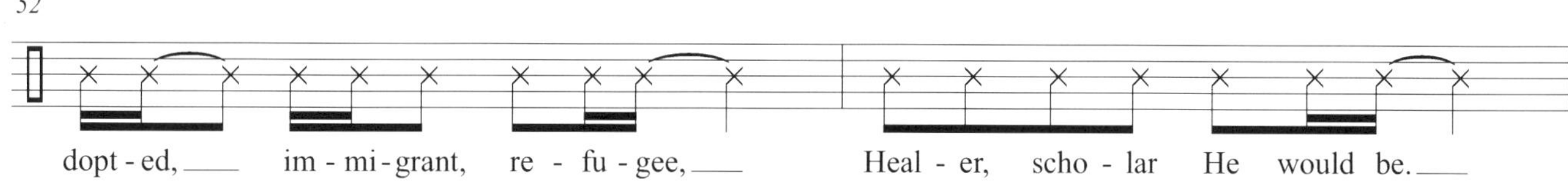

52
dopt - ed, im - mi - grant, re - fu - gee, Heal - er, scho - lar He would be.

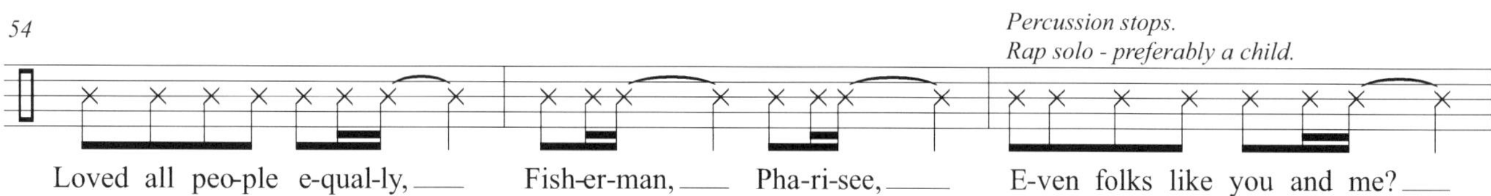

54
Percussion stops.
Rap solo - preferably a child.
Loved all peo - ple e - qual - ly, Fish - er - man, Pha - ri - see, E - ven folks like you and me?

Emmanuel Joy

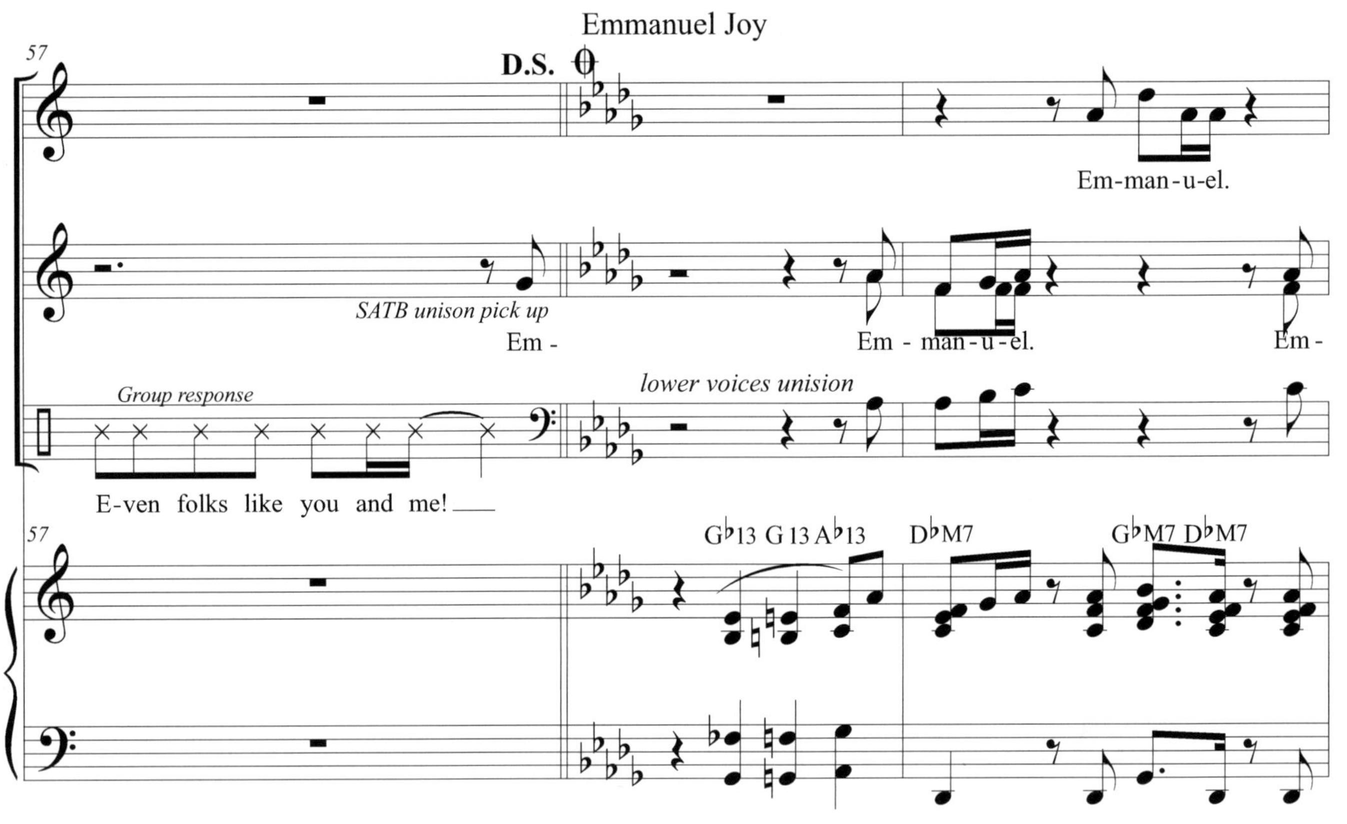

Emmanuel Joy

Enviado Soy de Dios - Each One of Us Is Sent
SAB/SATB and Congregation with optional panpipe/flute

Melody of hymn and Spanish text, traditional
Arr. with original material and English translation, A. Cáceres

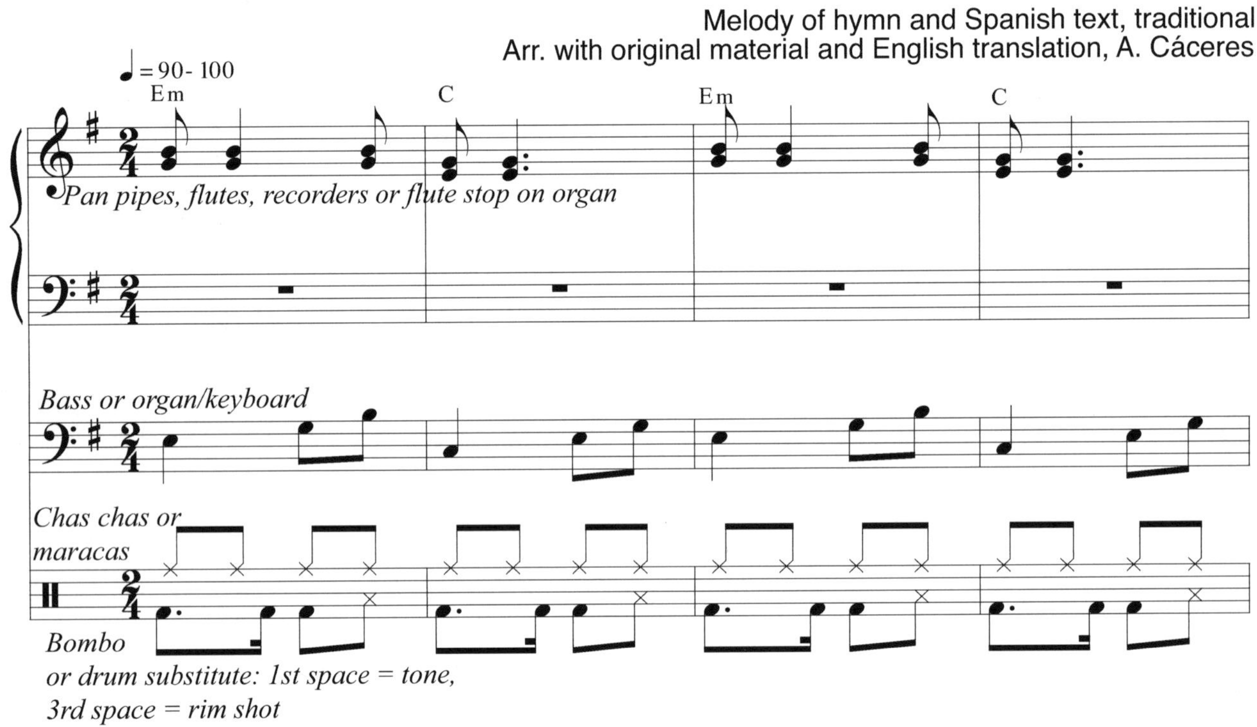

Please do not reproduce. Additional copies may be purchased from
World House Music, your local music or online retailer.
©2012 World House Music, Inc. www.worldhousemusic.org

24

Enviado Soy de Dios - Each One of Us Is Sent

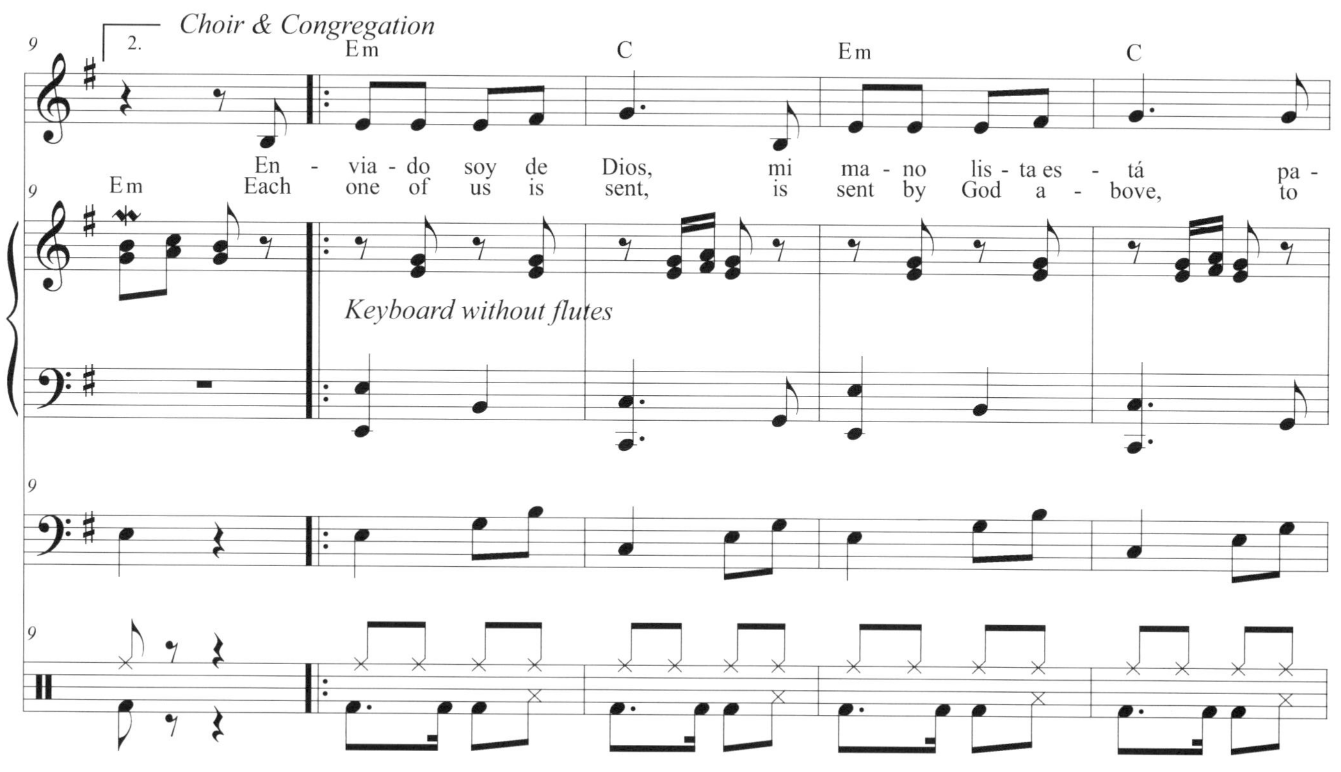

2.
Em   Am   D   G
nal.   Los án - ge - les no son sent   en - via - dos a cam -
love.   The an - gels are not   to do what we can
On repeat, ignore ties, play eighth notes

C   Am   B   Em
biar   un mun - do de do - lor   por un mun - do me -
do   to make a bet - ter world   for all, not just a

A m
D
G
jor;
few.
me ha to - ca - do a mí
It's up to you and me
ha - cer - lo rea - li -
to make the dream come

C
A m
B
1.
E m
dad.
true.
A - yú - da - me, Se - ñor,
We pray to you, O Lord,
a ha - cer tu vo - lun - tad.
to show us what to do.
Los
The

2. E m
tad.
do.
Flutes
C
Em
C

Am
B
Em

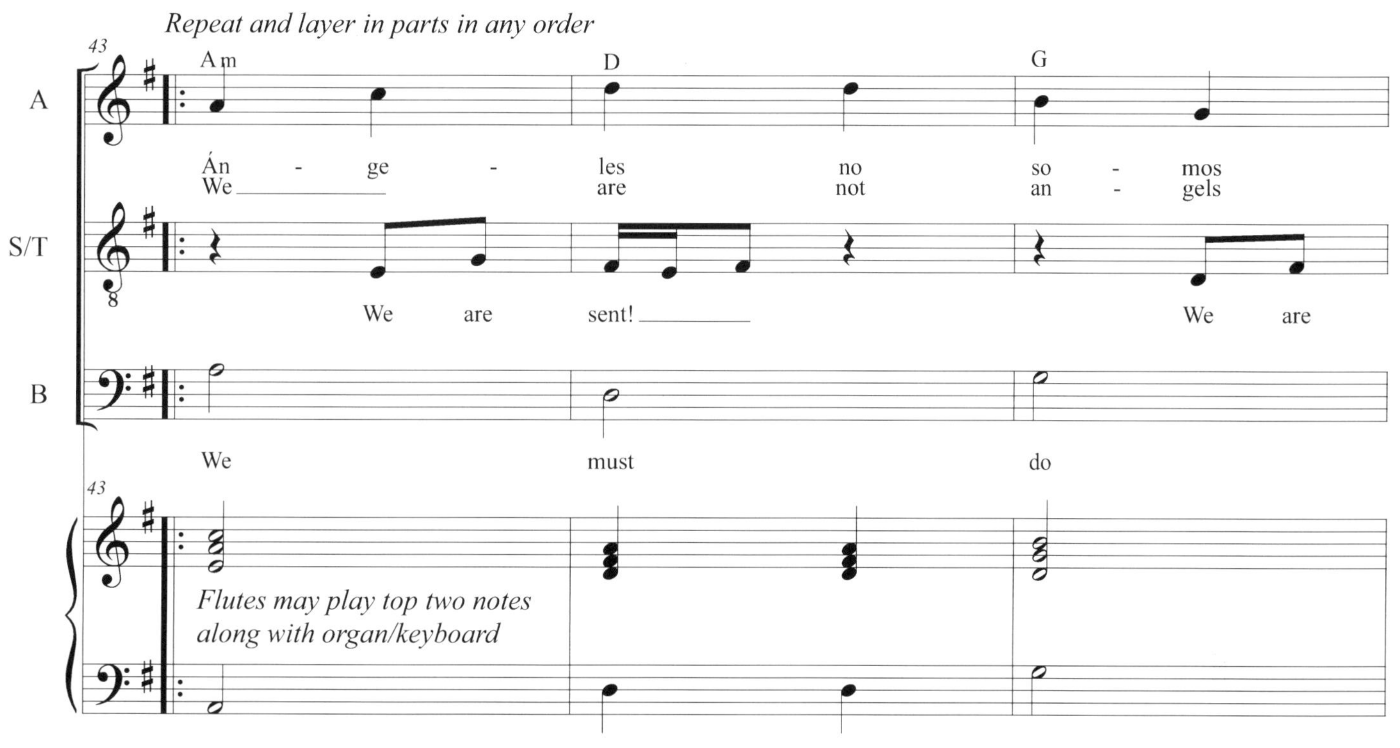
Repeat and layer in parts in any order
Am
D
G
A
Án - ge - les no so - mos
We are not an - gels
S/T
We are sent! We are
B
We must do
Flutes may play top two notes
along with organ/keyboard

C
Am
B
Em
A
pe - ro la ma - no lis - ta es - tá!
but we can do what we can do!
S/T
sent! We are sent to
B
what we can - - do!

Am
D
G
Án - ge - les no so - mos
We are not an - gels
be a - ga - pe love! We are sent! We are
Help to make

C
Am
B
Em
pe - ro la ma - no lis - ta es - tá!
but we can help the dream come true
sent! We are sent to love!
the dream come true!

Choir and Congregation
Em
C
Em
C
En - via - do soy de Dios, mi ma - no lis - ta es - tá, pa - to
Each one of us is sent, is sent by God a - bove, to
Flutes continue here
Em
Keyboard plays small notes if no flutes playing
Am
B
1. Em
2. Em
ra cons - truir con él un mun - do fra - ter - nal. En - nal. Los
do our ve - ry best to be a - ga - pe love. Each love. The

Enviado Soy de Dios - Each One of Us Is Sent
Sopranos & congregation
A m
D
G
án - ge - les no son en - via - dos a cam -
an - gels are not sent to do what we can -
Án - ge - les no so - mos
We are not an - gels
We are sent! We are
We must do
A capella on repeat
C
A m
B
biar un mun - do de do - lor por
do to make a bet - ter world for
pe - ro la ma - no lis - ta es -
but we can do what we can
sent! We are sent!
what we can -
33

un mun - do me - jor; me ha to - ca - do a mí ha -
all, not just a few. It's up to you and me to
tá! Án - ge - les no
do! We are not
to be a - ga - pe love! We are sent!
do! Help to
cer - lo rea - li - dad. A - yú - da - me, Se - ñor, a ha -
make the dream come true. We pray to you, O Lord, to
so - mos pe - ro la ma - no lis - ta es -
an - gels but we can help the dream come
We are sent! We are sent
make the dream

Em
Em Am Em Am Em B7 Em
cer tu vo - lun - tad. Los tad. La ma - no lis - ta es - ta!
show us what to do. The do. To make the dream come true!
tá! La ma - no lis - ta es - tá!
true! To make the dream come true!
to love! love! La ma - no lis - ta es - tá!
To make the dream come true!
- come true! true! La ma - no lis - ta es - tá!
To make the dream come true!
Flutes
8va

Fruit of the Spirit

SAB/SATB and Congregation

Abe Cáceres

Please do not reproduce. Additional copies may be purchased from
World House Music, your local music or online retailer.
©2012 World House Music, Inc. www.worldhousemusic.org

Fruit of the Spirit

Fruit of the Spirit

Fruit of the Spirit
Congregation in
E♭M9   A♭6   E♭M7   A♭6   B♭6   E♭sus4 E♭
Love.   Joy.   Peace.   Pa - tience. Kind - ness. Good-ness.
Gm   G   Cm   F9   B♭9   B♭ F/C D dim
Faith-ful -ness. Gen -tle-ness.   Self - con-trol.   Such are the fruit of the   Spi - rit.
E♭M9   A♭6   E♭M7   A♭6   B♭6   E♭sus4 E♭
Love.   Joy.   Peace.   Pa - tience. Kind - ness. Good-ness.

Unison voices
Higher voices
Gm   G   Cm   F 9   A♭M7/B♭
Faith - ful - ness. Gen - tle - ness.   Self - con-trol.   A - gainst   these   there   is   no
A - gainst   these____   no
E♭   A♭   E♭
law.   There   is   no   law.   A -
law.   There   is   no   law.

F 9
A♭M7/B♭
E♭
A♭
E♭
Congregation out
gainst these
there is no law.
There is no law.
A - gainst these___
no law.
There is no law.
A - gainst these___
(♭)
There is no
law!_______
___ no law!_______
Chord Gliss.
Chord Gliss.

I Am Available to You, O Lord

Unison or 2 Part Choir and Congregation

First time unison, second time in parts

Abe Cáceres

Inspired by a prayer by Pastor Reginald (Reggie) Hansome

42

I Am Available to You, O Lord

18
When singing in parts, top line
drops out for these 2 bars
A♭m
I am a - vail - a - ble.
I am a -
I am a - vail - a - ble.

High voices only
21
F m7
A♭/B♭ B♭7
E♭
B♭
E♭
D♭
vail - a - ble to You, O Lord.
I am a - Lord
to You, O
Lord.
Vamp as necessary
during prayers

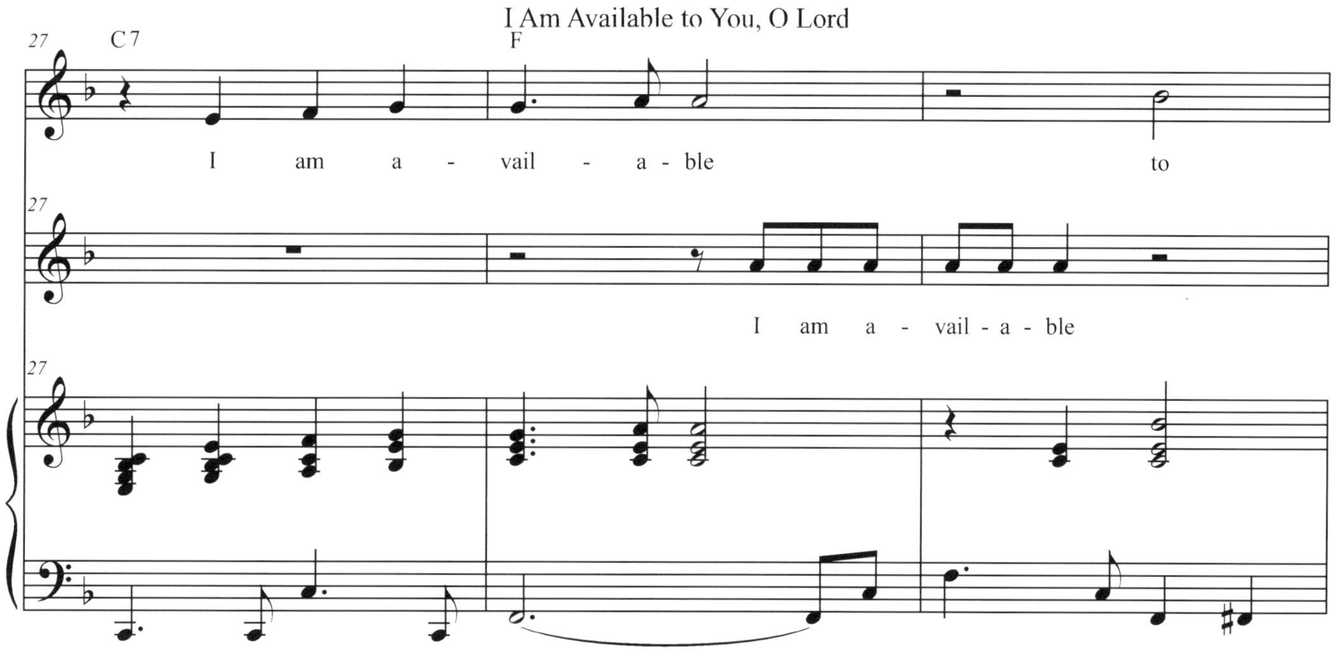
27
C 7
F
I am a - vail - a - ble
to
I am a - vail - a - ble

30
G m
C 7
A m/G G m
C
F
You.
I am a - vail - a-ble
to
You.
I am a-vail-a-ble to You.
I am a - vail-a-ble
I am a-vail-a-ble to

I Am Available to You, O Lord

I Am Available to You, O Lord

Somos Uno - We Are One

Also known as "Somos Uno en Cristo - We Are One in Christ"

Unison/SA/SAB/SATB with Congregation

Arranged with original material, A. Cáceres

worldhousemusic

Somos Uno - We Are One

Repeat first section if desired. Layer in the parts of next section as desired. Invite the congregation to sing one or more parts.
Additional possibilities are provided on final page and online at www.worldhousemusic.org. Feel free to make up your own
melodies with languages that reflect your region or area of ministry, or contact Dr. Abe to compose one for your congregation.

If playing as a *plena*, use the percussion break on lines 3 and 5: line 3 = bass on conga, line 5 = open tone on conga.

If playing as a *merengue*, use the percussion break on line 1; line 1 = open tone, x = rim shot or slap

Somos Uno - Languages

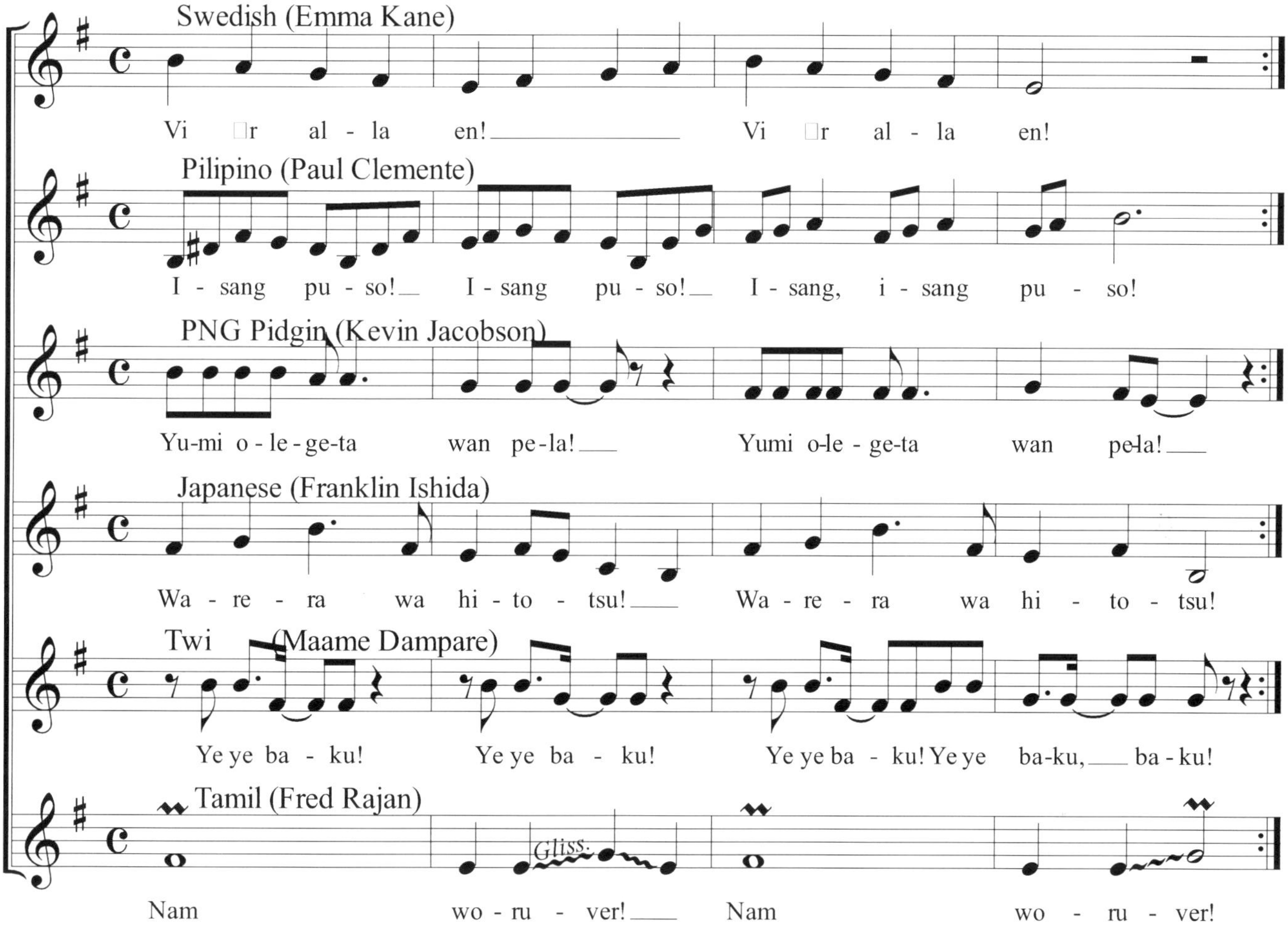

Here are some additional translations of the phrase, "we are one," or similar sentiment, each set
to a different melody. Check www.worldhousemusic.org for additional languages and melodies.

Please note the details below.
1. The literal translation for the Swedish is, "We are all one."
2. "Isang puso" in Pilipino means, "One heart."
3. The PNG Pidgin comes from, "You me altogether one fellow."
4. The Japanese is set to one of the traditional Japanese pentatonic scales.
5. Twi is a tonal language from Ghana. The pitches of the melody match the language tones.
6. The Tamil includes characteristic slides between pitches and melodic ornamentation.

Please do not reproduce. Additional copies may be purchased from World House Music, your local music or online retailer.
©2012 World House Music, Inc. www.worldhousemusic.org

glad in it! This is the Day of the Lord!

S
A/T
B
subito p
Unison choir, or if singing in parts, alto or tenor
subito p
subito p
subito p
The earth is the Lord's all,
The earth is the Lord's and the full - ness there - of, and all, all, all
The earth is the Lord's all, all

Optional soloist
This is the
S
all they __ that dwell there - in! Yes, This is the day!
(+ cong.)
f
A/T
__ they __ that dwell __ there - in! Yes, This is the day!
f
B
__ they __ that dwell there - in! Yes, This is the day!
f
day! ________ This ____ This is the day! ________
S
This is the day! This is the day that the Lord has __ made!
A/T
This is the day! This is the day Lord has made!
B
This is the day! This is the day Lord has made!

Re - joice! Re - joice!
Let us re - joice and be glad in it! This is the
Let us re - joice and be glad in it! This is the
Re - joice and re - joice and re - joice! This is the
day of the Lord! This is the day ho - ly day!
day of the Lord!
day of the Lord!
day of the Lord!
Choir only
This is the
This is the
This is the
Coda

This is the day, holy day!
day of the Lord!
Unison choir or altos
day of the Lord!
This is the day of the Lord!
day of the Lord!
Choir and congregation
ff
This is the day of the Lord! Re - joice! Re - joice! RE - JOICE!
This is the day of the Lord! Re - joice! Re - joice! RE - JOICE!
Re - joice! Re - joice! RE - JOICE!
This is the day of the Lord! Re - joice! Re - joice! RE - JOICE!
S
A/T
B

Index

Alphabetical

Old Testament

Psalms 118:24 and 24:1	This Is the Day
Psalm 133:1-3	All Are Welcome in This Place
Isaiah 64:8	I Am Available to You, O Lord

New Testament

Mathew 1:19-23; 2:13	Emmanuel Joy
Mathew 3:1-6, 13-17	El Bautismo (Baptism)
John 8:32	El Bautismo (Baptism)
Romans 12:9-11	All Are Welcome in this Place
Galatians 5:22-23	Fruit of the Spirit
Ephesians 2:4-18	All Are Welcome in this Place
Ephesians 4:2-6	Somos Uno – We Are One
Colossians 2:12	El Bautismo (Baptism)
James 2:14-17	Enviado Soy de Dios – Each One of Us is Sent

Interfaith

Psalms 118:24 and 24:1	This Is the Day
Isaiah 64:8	I Am Available to You, O Lord
Galations 5:22-23	Fruit of the Spirit
James 2:14-17	Enviado Soy de Dios – Each One of Us is Sent

About Dr. Abe

Abe Cáceres, also known as *Dr. Abe*, studied piano and organ at Syracuse University and holds a PhD in ethnomusicology from Indiana University. He is the Director of World House Music Inc., which promotes the joy and hope of peacemaking across cultural and religious boundaries through the magic of music and dance. His interactive programs of world music take place in schools, museums, churches, and interfaith venues. He is comfortable teaching activities as diverse as the Chinese Dragon dance, Afro-Latin percussion, piano and organ.

Active both as performer and composer, his songs and choral works have been performed on five continents. Dr. Abe accepts commissions to compose songs, anthems or instrumental works for special occasions. Visit our website for a list of compositions.

To book Dr. Abe for an event, contact:

worldhousemusic

www.worldhousemusic.org

Made in the USA
Columbia, SC
24 March 2022

57880899R00035